Mommy Moments

*Encouraging mothers on their mission
of motherhood*

Charlotte V. Murrell

xulon
PRESS

*I dedicate this book to the two
reasons that inspired me to write these
stories to begin with:
Jackson and Hannah*

Contents

Acknowledgements

Thanks to my God, Jesus Christ who gave me the talent to write my feelings down and gave me the never ending, burning desire and courage to take the necessary steps in seeing my work published. Thanks for making me a mommy, it is the highest honor.

To my wonderful partner, friend and love for my lifetime: Patrick who has encouraged and inspired me. You're love continues to overwhelm me. I'm so honored to be your wife. Thanks for being my biggest fan, believing in me and for telling, "you can".

To my loving, devoted mama and daddy, Marjorie and Marlin Vinson; your example in life has given me the courage to see my dreams come true. Your devotion and love towards me cannot be expressed in form of words. You have blessed my life so richly and I can never repay you for all that you have done. What an honor it is to be your daughter. I only hope that I can be to my children all that you have been to me.

To a friend that's truly a "God thing"; Laura Nelson. Your faith, prayers and encouragement overwhelm me. The love of Christ shines through you. Your friendship is so very valuable to me.

To a friend that truly gave me a huge nudge; Beth McCrabbs. Thanks girl! I finally did it.

To the MOPS group at my church; your prayers and excitement for me kept me inspired.

To many other friends who I could list but for fear I'd leave someone out I won't, but you know who you are. Thanks for the many prayers and words of encouragement. I hope you enjoy and keep passing on the treasures of a mother's heart.

To Xulon Press my publisher: Thanks for helping my dream come true.

And last to my two wonderful blessings, Jackson and Hannah, without you my life would be dull, there would be no stories to tell and I would not be the person I am today. Thank you for the love and life you bring to each new day. God has <u>big, big</u> plans for the two of you. *I love you.*

Introduction

For truly I say to you, if you have faith the size of a mustard seed,
you will say to this mountain move from here to there and it will
move and nothing will be impossible to you. Matthew 7:20

As a little girl I dreamed of being a mommy. I loved playing with baby dolls of any kind and my greatest joy as a child was the Christmas I received a doll called "Baby Alive". She could eat, drink and wet. I had hours of fun playing mommy with her. I also, remember a time my GA group from church went to a local children's home where children waited to be adopted. I remember not wanting to leave all those kids behind as we left. I just could not understand why they did not have a home to call their own. So to my own mother's dismay, I came home requesting that we go back and get all of them and bring them home with us. I was willing to share my room, my toys and do whatever I could to help. So, the desire to have a family to care for has been a growing desire of mine. Since then at times that desire caused great turmoil within my soul and I would find myself in deep thought; feeling emotions I did not know how to express any other way but in writing. So, at the tender age of seven I begin my life story of journaling. I wrote about anything and everything. Give me paper, a pen and a quite place and I get lost in another world – it's where God and I met.

Each of our lives is a story waiting to be told. The stories I share in this book did not come from me, I have to give credit to the one true author, my heavenly Father, he's the author of all things. I simply have taken a talent he gave me long ago and have built on it so that I can offer my works up to him as a praise offering. I prayfully chose stories that had the strongest impact in my life. Some I struggled with revealing, because they are very personal but very real. But, God said they needed to be told (that means that somebody out there needs to buy this book (☺), so here they are, the good, the bad and the ugly. In my writing I try to capture my children's personalities and the different stages of their lives especially the way they talk. So, in some stories words will not be gramatically correct and I have done this on purpose to capture the moment. This is the real thing and I desire for each story to bless you and encourage you in your own life and how God has delicately woven his plan for you into each day. Now, begin the journey of each day a mother spends caring for her family and walking with Jesus as she shares her moments in mothering.

Opening Prayer

*A*s I sit here on a "very small" bench in my kitchen on the 2nd day of April, sun shining, birds singing, my thoughts have <u>only</u> been interrupted six times in the past five minutes. I wonder what I could say to a mother who has just picked up this book to read hoping to catch a gleam of hope, a word of encouragement or just a little laugh about the ups and downs of being a mother. I too, have gone in bookstores looking for hope, for encouraging words and answers about being a mother. I carefully chose entries from my personal journals that might touch the hearts of mothers, make you laugh and cry and say I can identify with that. So to all us mommies out there "this prayer is for you."

Oh Lord, today there's so much to do on my" to do list" that I don't even have time to make my list, nor do I know where to find a piece of unused paper to write upon. But you Lord, know my thoughts, my fears, my struggles and you will guide me on my journey today. Lord my cup may be almost empty as I hear my name called once again by someone who is in need, but I know you can fill my cup where I will never thirst again. Shine through me and strengthen me for my many tasks today for you blessed me and made me a mother and with you, I can be a mother today. Amen.

The Invitation

This is a formal invitation to you from <u>God</u>:
You have specifically been chosen to receive this invitation to be a mother.
When: Upon the birth of your child
Time: 24 hours a day
        Seven days a week
        365 days a year
Place: Everywhere you go

God honorable invites you to become a mother and change a life forever.

Have you ever really thought about what it means to be a mother? Wow! What an awesome responsibility. Every time a child is born so is a mother. God handpicked you even me to be a mother. What an honor!!! I hope you will enjoy motherhood as much as I have and continue to. Now let the journey begin.

My frame was not hidden from You, when I was made in secret, and skillfully wrought in the depths of the earth; Your eyes have seen my unformed substance; and in Your book were all written the days that were ordained for me, when as yet there was not one of them. Psalm 139:15-16

Blessed

*She opens her mouth in wisdom, and the teaching of kindness
is on her tongue. She looks well to the ways of her household...
Her children rise up and bless her... Proverbs 31:26-28*

She's called "cool" by her 5 year old.

She's often told "You're the bestest mama ever" by her 3 year old.

She's given a wink and a thumbs up across the playground.

She's told she smells like a "mommy".

She's asked the critical questions like: When we let the water out of
the tub do we drown the worms in the ground? Where does the
sun sleep at night? Does God know how to swim? Did you love
daddy first?

She's given a child's favorite pillow when she's sick.

Her daughter names all her dolls after her.

Her son's best debate statement is: "Well, my mommy said".

Her child's face lights up when she walks into a room.

Her voice and touch are the last request from tiny ones at the close of each day.

Her name is called more than any other word in the history of language.

Her daughter mimics her actions in her make believe world.

Her son seeks her approval often.

So often these small things go unnoticed by her through the days, for she is ever busy serving, caring, and planning for her family but; when time is taken these are the things that can be recalled for these are the things that go before her and go behind her in her children. Yes, these are the ways her children rise up and call her blessed.

I thought it would be a long time before my children would rise up and call me blessed like the verse mentions. But as I begin to take notice to the things my children did that made me happy and feel loved I begin to see all the many ways and times they were currently rising up and blessing me. I can't help but beam with joy when I think of the look on my Jackson's face when he sees me across the playground, or getting off the bus after school. His little face just lights up like a big Christmas tree. That blesses me more than words can ever express because I know that I've made an impression on his heart. He knows when he sees mama everything's all right. I wouldn't have it any other way.

<u>Moment of Encouragement</u>

Today think of some things your children do to rise up and bless you. Make a list and put in on the mirror in your bathroom; that way you will see it often.

<u>Moment with the Father</u>

Heavenly Father, I'm so grateful that you blessed me with two children. Thank you for helping me see the different ways they bless me each day. I want to continue to be the kind of mother that teaches them and comforts them. Help me learn better ways to mother them and place other women in my life to guide me and be a mentor to me. Amen.

Who am I?

For am I now seeking, the favor of or of God? Or am I striving to please men? If I were still trying to please men, I would not be a bondservant of Christ. Galatians 1:10

*L*ord, I've fallen and I can't get up (the truth be told I don't want to have to get up). I've failed at this motherhood thing. I just don't get it! I don't feel like a mother. I feel more like a maid and short order cook. I've lost my motivation and the joy of mothering is long gone. So here I am before you, Lord. I've lost myself – the who I am- my dreams and personal goals, I don't know what they are anymore. My goals now consist of getting through the day without yelling at the kids, fixing three meals (5 meals if you count snacks), washing, cleaning, nursing, bathing, fixing, washing and washing. I'm not ready to face the two faces outside these doors. I want to run and hide for the rest of the day.

Then a still small voice revealed to me:

-You've fallen but there's no place too deep that I

can't reach you.

-You've lost yourself but I come that you might be found.

-You've sacrificed your dreams but I prepare a table of blessings before you.

-You feel you can't face your responsibilitics that await you but I am your strength and light.

-You are weary and I come to be your hiding place.

-I'm all you really need and I'm here for you always.

Moment of Encouragement

Ever had a day like this one? Maybe today you are, likely somewhere out there some poor mother has "fallen" at this very moment. As mothers we are entitled to a few bad days. It's hard to face the same chores over and over day after day. Take your weariness, lack of excitement, and loneliness to Jesus Christ. He's always with you even when you don't feel his presence.

Moment with the Father

Heavenly Father, today I'm struggling at being the kind of mother you desire of me. Give me strength, patience and ease the loneliness I feel. Help me to feel your presence in my life today and meet the needs I have so that I might be able to meet the needs of my family. Amen

Happy New Year

*And I shall give them one heart,
and put a new spirit
within them. Ezekiel 11:19*

"What's a new year?" asked Jackson.

"Well, it's a time when our calendar of months starts over and we begin again, except we begin as a new year," I explained.

"What's a revolution?" he asked.

"Do you mean a resolution?" I questioned more, knowing he had recently heard about New Year's resolutions.

"Yeah," he smiled.

"Well, at the start of a new year people like to think of several things they would like to improve for the next year, and those things are called New Year's resolutions. A new year is like getting a fresh start, a new beginning for people," I responded.

"Oh, so if you messed up the year before you get to start again and make things better," he said.

"Yeah, you've got the right idea," I replied.

That small conversation got me to really thinking how funny it is how we get stuck on making New Year's resolutions. It's like we never think of making a fresh start any other time during the year except January 1. Why is it that we wait until then to begin again? Why don't we try to improve our lives each day? God gives us a fresh beginning each new day we are able to wake up. Whatever we did the day before is over and done with in God's eyes and He's ready for us to begin again. He's always there waiting and willing to forgive and wash away our sins, to bring us a new hope, a new peace and a new beginning.

Moment of Encouragement

Maybe today you got up and your day started out all wrong, now's the perfect time to ask Jesus to give you a fresh start. Maybe today you've already gone to him five times so what's holding you back from making it six? It's ok!!! We all have days that we need lots of fresh starts throughout our day. That doesn't makes us any less of a good mother, in fact it can and will make you a better mother. Just think of the example you are setting for your children.

Moment with the Father

Heavenly Father, so many days we need to come to you and ask for forgiveness but we don't. I'm sure you get frustrated when we try to manage things ourselves and play the role of "Mr. Fix-it". Today I come before you asking you to forgive me for _____. I need a fresh start. I need your understanding. I need your peace. I need you to give me a new beginning. Amen.

M-O-T-H-E-R

*B*eing the mother of a toddler and a blooming preschooler can be most challenging and very tiring; so after a long day of hearing my name called more than I wanted to hear it; I took time to think about what the word "mother" means to this group of children.

M is for more, more and more

O is for octopus (you will wish you were one with extra hands to carry things, open doors as you balance a toddler on one hip, carry a diaper bag, a purse, a security toy, and hold the hand of a preschooler)

T is for transformer (you'll learn quickly how to change from being a nurse, to a party planner, to a teacher, to a walking trash can and human Kleenex)

H is for hunger the one thing that <u>will</u> happen 5 minutes after the

kitchen is completely clean

E is for escort (you will have one where ever you go, whether you want one or not)

R is for refuge (you will be the one your child runs to when he/she needs protection; and what a privilege that is as a mother).

Moment of Encouragement

Being a mother is the hardest yet most rewarding job we can have. It takes great courage to be a mother and do it full time. It is often scary and lonely. Don't let the day to day chores of mothering rob you of the honors God has in store for you.

Moment with the Father

Heavenly Father, you know the challenges I face being a mother. Be near me as I provide for my children, make the necessary changes that are required and let me find joy in my "free escort service" while the time allows; because I know the day will come when I will long to have a small child on my heels. Thank you for the honor and gift to be a mother. Help me see the rewards you have in store for me during each day. Amen

My Gifts to You During the Toddler Years

Every good thing given and every perfect gift
is from above, coming down from the Father
of lights, with whom there is no variation
or shifting shadow. James 1:17

*H*ow convicting this verse hit me today. I began to think about what kind of gifts I was giving Jackson who has just turned 8 months old. Are they gifts that would honor God? So I came up with a list of things I wanted to achieve.

To give you space to learn to walk and hold your hand until you're sure.

Offer words of praise in your presence upon the arrival of your big accomplishment and shed my tears in private, of baby of mine who has grown to be a toddler in such a short time.

To take a daily course in baby babble and be your personal interpreter for the rest of the world.

To pray before each meal is eaten to teach you to be grateful for the food you have and to thank God for providing your needs.

To kneel by your crib in the middle of the night and thank God for his blessings and to say "thank you" to you for sharing the day with me.

To kiss your daddy daily in front of you so you never fear that your tiny world is safe and secure.

To roll on the floor and laugh with you to teach you I'm still a kid too.

To kneel down at your eye level when you talk to me and I to you to show you how important you are.

To read you bible stories to teach you that Jesus is real and he cares for you.

To let you run, scream, kick things, and throw things (sometimes) to let you know it's ok to just be a kid.

To set boundaries and rules for your safety and well being but to enforce these is most important of all.

To cuddle with you in the middle of the day to show you I have time for you and I enjoy your company.

To love you unconditionally so that you know, that this kind of love is not extinct.

Moment of Encouragement

Take the time to think about what gifts you want to give your child each day. These gifts will change as the seasons of your child's life changes. It's a priceless treasure to keep a written list to look back on as your child grows; you will see that you have also grown.

Moment with the Father

Heavenly Father, thank you for the many gifts you give to each one of us to use to honor you. Thank you for the greatest gift you gave us – everlasting life. Let the gifts I choose to give my child be pleasing to you. Amen.

My Little Thank You's

The Lord has done great things for us;
we are glad. Psalm 126:3

I try to see every day life through my children's eyes. You would be amazed at how small and insignificant our grown-up troubles can be. So here's a glimpse into a child's world at the ways he/she might say "thank you" to <u>YOU</u> for being a mommy.

The sound of pitter-patter feet in the early morning.
The imprints of messy hands gone unwashed left behind on windows and doors.
Tiny cars and trucks lined up and arranged to resemble a mini city of make believe.
Tiny doll shoes and dress up clothes strode around in the after math of pretend fairy tale princesses who live happily ever after.
The distinct tone of a tiny voice that calls 'mommy' over 20 times in one day.

The tiny hand that holds mine sometimes resistant, sometimes with great strength.

Innocent eyes that are always watching and learning.

The sound of sweet dreams and the look of peace and contentment on a small face as it sleeps.

The silence of bedtime as everyone sleeps.

These are my little thank yous to you mommy for all you do for me, because I'm much to small to tell you in other ways I do my best to show you in ways you will remember I know you care.

Moment of Encouragement

Have you thought that your toddler might want to say thank you to you but just can't. As mothers we don't hear thank you very often especially not from infants, toddlers or preschoolers. However, I believe when you begin teaching kindness and gentleness at the infancy stage, kids learn what it means to be grateful towards others. When my children are happy and carefree I know that they feel secure and feel loved and I know that I helped make their surroundings secure enough for them to feel that way. Think about it and pat yourself on the back for a job well done.

Moment with the Father

Heavenly Father, Thank you for your love and the ways you care for me. Help me to not take you for granted. Amen

A Hairy Situation

But the very hairs of your head are all numbered;
so do not fear; you are more valuable than many sparrows.
Matthew 10:30-31

*I*t's been several months ago that a very traumatic accident happened that I thought I would never be able to talk about; but with God's gracious hand upon the situation I can now find some humor in that day. It all began with a mother and daughter making a cake for daddy. So many, many times this duo had worked together making cakes and enjoyed getting messy and tasting the cake batter along the way. Today was no different and carefully measuring and pouring mother and daughter were well on their way to having the perfect cheesecake just like daddy loved. So as I handed Hannah the last cup of sugar to pour into the mixing bowl, I turned to the side to grab an egg and suddenly I heard a very sharp scream and a very strange sound come from the mixer. I turned around to find my daughter's head in the mixing bowl with her hair wrapped tightly around the beaters in the mixer. I froze - for how long I do not know, but I was horrified at what I saw. I reached for the bowl to unhook it from the rest of the mixer and took Hannah in my arms. Amazingly I did not have to untwist her mangled hair but as I inspected her head I found a large bare spot on top of her head and quickly glanced back at the mixer to see her hair attached. She cried and I cried. I tried to comfort her best I could but I was beside myself with grief. Within minutes Hannah was running around playing unharmed by what had just happened. Myself, well I was a mess. I tearfully untangled my sweet baby girl's curls of hair and held it in my hands and sobbed. How could I have been so stupid to take my eyes off of her? What kind of mother am I? How am I going to explain this to my dear husband and what will people say when they see her? Oh yeah, the guilt flowed in like a huge tidal wave drowning me. I found myself alone and afraid. Hannah came back into the kitchen where I was sobbing and asked if we could finish the cake for daddy. I took one look at her and all I could see was that huge bare spot on her head and I grabbed her and said, "I'm so sorry you got your hair pulled." She just smiled and said, "It no hurts no more." In her world all was right but in mine all was a mess. I tried to call my husband who was working but could get no answer. I then called my dear mother whose voice was a lifeline for me at this moment. I explained the accident between sobs and she reassured me, as any mother would do for her child. So I was able to pull my emotions together and get our mess cleaned up. I managed to savage the cake and finish it. " More than love went into making this cake", I thought as I put it into the frig.

In the next few days that followed this incident I almost could not bear to look at Hannah without crying but with God's hand in my life he began to show me I'm never alone. Children can teach you some wonderful things that we as adults take for granted in the bible. My son Jackson came and told me: "Mommy, you know when Hannah lost her hair, did you know that God had to recount all her hair? He knows how many hairs are in your head all the time that's really neat huh?" I pondered that for several days. At first I thought, "this is not funny God and if you're using my son to try and shed some humor on the situation it's not working." But God did not give up on me. Again my son approached me. "Mommy, how long do you think it takes God to count to a trillion? he asked. "Not very long." I replied. "Why do you ask?" I said. "Just curious 'cause I've tried to count Hannah's hair and I can't do it, she won't be still." he replied. "I bet God can just look at you and know how many hairs you have. He must think you're really special to do that, huh mommy?" He said smiling.

"Yeah, he must." I said. Yeah, if God cares about the hairs on my head he certainly cares about me as a person and he still thinks I'm a good mother and so should I.

Moment of Encouragement

There are all times in our mothering years we wish we could do things differently. Like the saying that goes "If I only knew then what I know now." But good news, Jesus Christ loves you and thinks you're very special despite past, present and future mistakes.

Moment with the Father

Heavenly Father, thank you for caring for me above the birds of the air. Thank you for being near me during this tragic accident and for allowing me to find some humor in the situation. Amen

Say it, Aloud

*"Pleasant words are a honeycomb, sweet to the soul
and healing to the bones." Proverbs 16:24*

*"Bright eyes gladden the heart;
Good news puts fat on the bones." Proverbs 15:30*

*"A soothing tongue is a tree of life.
But perversion in it crushes the spirit." Proverbs 15:4*

Quietness. There are times my whole body screams out for it. I'm an introvert (we live for complete quietness; we get re-energized by being alone) and I live with three extroverts (THEY need lots of activity and noise, they get re-energized by being around others and doing) so do you get the picture? I'm way out numbered. I live in a house of chaos (just kidding, guys). Though it is hard to get past all the demands and needs of others, as mothers we need to push past all other powers that be and speak calming, uplifting words to ourselves. Have you ever really thought about that? Have you ever tried it?

Just picture this scenario:

You're washing dishes, the kids are playing in the kitchen, suddenly, someone wants a drink, then someone else needs help "going potty" and you begin to say aloud, "How precious are your thoughts of me, O God! How vast is the sum of them! If I were to count them they would outnumber the sand. For You did not give {me} a spirit of timidity, but a spirit of power, of love and of self-discipline."

Here's a list of positive, uplifting words you can say to yourself to offer encouragement:

- ♥ I will not become weary. I will reap my harvest in _____ if I do not give up.
- ♥ God is a shield about me.
- ♥ God is my present help.
- ♥ God is at my right hand and I will not be shaken.
- ♥ God is faithful.
- ♥ God will never let me go.
- ♥ God is intimately acquainted with me.
- ♥ God will accomplish what concerns me.
- ♥ I am the head and not the tail; I shall be above and not beneath.
- ♥ God delights in me.
- ♥ God will make me glad.
- ♥ God is my shelter.
- ♥ I'm a beautiful woman.
- ♥ I'm a loving wife.
- ♥ I'm a dedicated mother.
- ♥ I do a wonderful job.
- ♥ God delights in me. God delights in Me. God delights in ME!

<u>Moment of Encouragement</u>

There's a saying that goes, "If mama ain't happy, nobody's happy." Well, there's a lot of truth to that. We have power to set the tone for our home. We can speak negative words or we can speak positive words. Satan does not want you to uplifted and joyful despite what is going on around you. That's why it's so important for us to speak good into our lives and speak them aloud. If you seek quietness, you can find it within as you say it aloud.

Moment with the Father

Gracious Heavenly Father, How great you are and how awesome it is that you love me so. It's hard for me to comprehend your knowledge and wisdom. Put before me daily reflections of your thoughts of me. Amen.

Fabric Softener

*For we are a fragrance
of Christ to God
among those who are being
saved and among those
who are perishing. 2 Corinthians 2:13*

I had already washed three loads of clothes, had two more to wash and four loads to fold and one to dry. How can one family of four get so dirty? I piled the clothes to fold in the middle of the living room floor and called for all hands to come help. "We're having a laundry party!" I announced.

"Yeah! What's a laundry party?" asked Jackson racing to see what was happening.

"It's a party held once a week to help mothers fold all the clean clothes," I replied jokingly.

"That's not funny, Mama," replied Jackson.

"Well, it was to me," I said.

I started the kids folding washcloths and sorting socks. I returned to the laundry room to start the load of clothes in the dryer. When I returned to the living room I found my daughter dressed with her brother's batman underwear as a skirt, her daddy's socks as gloves and my bra as a hat. What a site!! (Picture time)

"These mell so wcet," she said.

"Mama makes them that way," shared my son.

"They soft too," she added.

"Mama make them like that too," continued my son. (Quiet an interesting conversation going on here.) "First, she washes them to get all the dirt out then she puts perfume in 'em and then cooks 'em until they're like new again. Right Mama?" explained Jackson.

"Something like that," amazed at the grow-up conversation I was hearing go on between a nineteen month old and a three year old.

What an glorious lesson I learned by allowing my children to help with a simple chore.

God deals with a lot of laundry in our lives too. He sorts us through trials, washes our sins away daily, spins us to purify our souls, adds his touch of grace as softener to the fabric of our hearts. Do my children smell the sweetness of God's love in my speech? Do they feel the softness of God's love in my touch? Does God's spirit of freshness linger in my child's lives even when I'm not there?

Moment of Encouragement

Definitely, gives you something to think about. A life-changing lesson learned by doing a simple chore such as folding clothes. Get your kids involved in chores around the house. Even a two year old can do things like empty trashcans, water small plants, fed pets, wipe table and chairs. I try to make it exciting and funny that way I get everyone's cooperation and we're able to have lots of life changing lessons and the chores get done too.

Moment with the Father

Heavenly Father, I thank you for your grace and mercy. I thank you for this lesson I learned from my children. I pray you will give me the insight to see the impurities in my life. Help me to come clean before you. Show me creative ways to teach my children about you and let the fragrance of Christ Jesus linger in our home. Amen.

Be Angry but Don't Sin

*"Be angry, and yet do not sin do not let the sun go down
On your anger." Ephesians 4:26*

*B*e angry and sin not! Surely that verse was not intended for mothers of 2 year olds. What's the deal with the attitude and whining about EVERYTHING? Don't even get me started on the disobeying and the flopping on the floor, breath holding, screaming and kicking, "nobody loves me" temper tantrums. You won't believe what happen today when I told him he had to turn the TV off? He wet on the TV remote! He stood there in MY living room and wet on the TV remote. (How do you sanitize that?) Well, I counted to 10, maybe to fast but it never works anyway these days. The next thing I know he's cheering, "Mommy, mommy, wook I go tee-tee, see. I get candy?" We're trying the potty thing, can you tell? I had to laugh. It was priceless. I could just see this being played as a Hallmark commercial for Mother's Day. Anyway, later he really got to me when he took handfuls of his lunch and dropped it on the floor. How ungrateful can a child be? I worked hard to prepare a healthy lunch for him. Well, I lost it at that point. My tolerance had run out, I personally blame it on "being with child #2". I screamed and stomped my feet (basically had my very own adult fit) and put him in his room. I'm tired of saying, "don't do that, don't do this, and don't touch that, stop that, stand up, sit still, be quiet." (You feel my pain at this point don't you?) I feel like a sergeant instead of a mother. He's so impatient, so impolite, so demanding, so innocent, so fun, so loveable, so moldable, and so teachable. I guess I didn't teach him much about patience and self-control today. Forgive me, forgive me Lord. It's so hard these days to be angry and sin not.

Moment of Encouragement

There's definitely a change that occurs when a child turns two or is it the mommy who changes and no one has figured that out until now? I'll have to ponder that one a bit longer but changes do occur around this time that none of us want to deal with day in and day out. However, let me encourage you to take notice of this season as a growing time, a teaching time and a bonding time. Discover something funny about your day and laugh.

Moment with the Father

Most gracious Heavenly Father, thank you for giving me patience to mother during the toddler years. This is such a funny time in my child's life where he does some really outrageous things. Sometimes I think we could provide energy to the whole world using all the 2 year olds. His energy never runs out and yet mine has. Give me strength and rest my soul. Help me find the fun along the way and make time to laugh. Amen

What Did You do Today?

I will instruct you and teach you in the way which you should go; I will counsel you with My eye upon you. Psalm 32:8

She wakes early while the house is totally silent and she listens. Oh, the peace that fills this place. She quietly goes from room to room checking her little ones; oh the content that fills their faces. She looks at the clock, her time is running short so she sits and looks out the window at the wonder of another day and she begins to talk with Jesus. "Thank you for the night's rest and for another day, thank you for your protection and for this beautiful sunrise. Thank you for my Patrick, Jack-

"Mommy!! Good morning." interrupts her son as he runs to awaiting arms for his morning hug. "Mama, I firsty." he said.

"Lord, I'll get back with you, can you wait for me?" she whispers under her breath as she gets up to attend to her family's needs.

"Honey, do you know where my blue socks are?" ask her husband.

"Yes, honey," she starts to reply but is quickly interpreted by her son.

"Mama, mama I firsty."

"Mama, mama, I eat" cries out her daughter.

"OK. Just a minute, daddy needs me," she shares with her children as her husband calls out once again.

"Honey!" "I'm coming!" she replies. "Wait for me Lord, I'll be back." she breaths.

"Here's your socks, sweetheart. Good morning. I'll get your coffee to you, the kids are hungry so give me a chance to attend to them and I'll be back" she responds.

"MAMA!" cries somebody from the kitchen.

"I'M COMING!!" she shouts back.

Fixing breakfast she see the chores that need to be done and begins to make a priority list in her mind: *wash clothes, pay bills, clean frig——-*

Getting the kids breakfast she begins to wash dishes; "Mama, Hannah spilt her juice" brags her son.

"Oh, Hannah sweetie don't play in it" she said as she begins to clean up.

"I do it, mine" screams her daughter wanting to do things herself.

"Honey, I'm going off to work, have a good day, I love you" states her husband as he heads out the door.

"Bye, have a great day. I love you, too" she responds back.

She takes care of spills, changes diapers, calms an angry toddler declaring independence, helps a preschooler tie his shoes, fills juice cups, washes clothes, plays a game of hide-n-seek while making beds, pays a few bills between Barney and Clifford, holds a toddler while she makes a few phone calls, reads fourteen stories, sings seven songs and answers sixty-two questions all before lunch.

"Lord, I promise I haven't forgot you, I've just been real busy" she whispers aloud.

"Mama, what's for lunch?" ask her son.

"I'm getting to it, kids. Just be patient." she huffs.

After lunch, she changes diapers, more stories are told, trips to the potty, gets dirty dishes in sink and hooray its naptime!!!

Once more quietness fills this place.

"Lord, I'm back. Thanks for waiting. Oh, what a day it's been. I'm so tired, so lonely and feel so inadequate to handle this job you've given me" she begins as she pours her heart out to Jesus.

"You're never alone. I've been right by you throughout your day. I've watched you comfort your crying child, I've watched you help your child tie his shoes, I've watched you tenderly and effortlessly fix meals, say blessings of thanks and oversee lessons of kindness, self-control, manners and brotherly love. You've selflessly given yourself to these young ones as their demands grew so did your care for them. I noticed each step you took today. Even as you do for your family so you are doing for me. I'm very proud of you and I love you," replied Jesus.

Moment of Encouragement

It is all to easy for us as mothers to get caught up in the demands of our day that we forget God is aware of our rising up and our sitting down. He notices all the small things we do that no one else does and he knows how we long to rest in his arms. So if all you have time for is to breathe his name then just inhale.

Moment with the Father

Heavenly Father, my time is very limited today as you are aware. I do long to spend time in your presence, to rest in your arms and wait on you but my days demands out number the minutes in my day so I ask for your guidance and strength as I mother today. Give me joy and make me glad. Amen.

Common Words We Share

*All those who had believed were together and had
all things in common. Acts 2:44*

I cannot believe how many times I have repeated myself today. I secretly planted a tape recorder to record my day. Here are some of the things I caught myself saying:

♥ Sit on your bottom in that chair.
♥ Use your napkin not your sleeve.
♥ Flush the toilet.
♥ Did you wash your hands?
♥ Keep your hands and feet to yourself.
♥ Sit down.
♥ Remember your manners.
♥ Use words to tell me.
♥ Don't whine.
♥ I don't understand whining.

♥ Don't spit.
♥ Say excuse me.
♥ Don't run with that in your mouth.
♥ Don't chase your sister.
♥ Don't play so rough.
♥ Put your shoes back on.
♥ What did you say?
♥ Don't sit so close to the TV.
♥ That's too loud.
♥ Go potty before we leave.
♥ Try to go anyway.
♥ Just go try!
♥ I'm waiting.
♥ I'm still waiting.
♥ We're waiting on you.
♥ Hurry up.
♥ Buckle your seat belt.
♥ No screaming in the van.
♥ Don't make me pull over.
♥ Wait 'til we get home.
♥ No, you cannot go swimming in the winter.
♥ Summer is four months away.
♥ Yes, I do care.
♥ No! And that's final.
♥ You don't know what boring is.
♥ Go outside.
♥ Close the door.
_I'm on the phone.
♥ Just a minute.
♥ Keep that in the kitchen.
♥ Close the refrigerator.
♥ She had it first.
♥ Share.
♥ Because that's what we do in our family.
♥ Did you hear me?
♥ Then answer me.
♥ Don't make me repeat myself.

- ♥ What do you need?
- ♥ Use an inside voice.
- ♥ What are you doing up?
- ♥ Maybe.
- ♥ I'll let you know.
- ♥ Go back to bed.
- ♥ Do you want a spanking?
- ♥ Whose is this?
- ♥ Where does it go?
- ♥ Don't use that tone with me.
- ♥ Be careful.
- ♥ Don't go near the road.
- ♥ Play where I can see you.
- ♥ Wait for everyone else.
- ♥ Close your eyes when we pray.
- ♥ Come to the table.
- ♥ This is the third call for dinner.
- ♥ Try again.
- ♥ I'm proud of you.
- ♥ Look what you can do.
- ♥ Good job.
- ♥ I need a kiss.
- ♥ You're so funny.
- ♥ I love you.

Sound familiar? Did you find yourself smiling? We all share a common language in our mothering. Some days we have more patience than others, some days we find creative ways to inspire our children and other days we just do what needs to be done to survive.

Moment of Encouragement

As women of Christ we can share a common language with God – prayer. Through prayer we can turn the stresses of our day over to God; allow him to turn things around for us and change us from the inside out. We can join together in bible study groups, women conferences, playgroups, and various other socials to encourage one another. As mothers we can feel free to share our stories and trust that others will understand – cause most of us have been there, done that, and said that.

Moment with the Father

Heavenly Father, thank you for the common bonds women share as mothers. I'm glad I can laugh at some of the things I say to my kids day after day. But, do not let me forget to share with you daily. I so much desire to keep my relationship with you on track so that we work on the same plans together. Amen.

Unconditional Love

"Love is patient, love is kind and is not jealous, love does not brag and is not arrogant, does not act unbecomingly; it does not seek its own, is not provoked, does not take into account a wrong suffered, does not rejoice in unrighteousness, but rejoices with the truth; bears all things, believes all things, hopes all things, endures all things. Love never fails..." 1 Corinthians 13:4-8

Sometimes as mothers we end up being what I call "married single moms"; meaning that our husband's work takes him away from the family a lot and we end up being the sole caregiver to our little ones. So, if you're one of the few, courageous somewhat insane women to go it alone; then you can definitely identify with this story. This is one encounter of nine days without my husband who was out of town on business. It's time for bed and I am way past the point of being ready to get the kids in bed when the following happens:

"Mommy, can you turn my music tape over?" called my 5-year-old son.

"In a minute," I responded.

"Mommy weed a story?" asked my 3-year-old daughter.

"Ok, but just one, mommy is very tired tonight," I answered.

"Mommm! I need my tape turned over," called my son.

"OK! I'll be there in a minute!" I shouted. I was getting impatient with all the demands of the day piling up, and I was alone to handle all their requests. Can't they see I'm trying to do the best I can? It's bedtime and everyone needs something. I was so exhausted. All I wanted to have was some time to myself, a bit of peace and quiet. But the kid's demands outweighed my needs. They kept needing and wanting. Usually, I looked forward to putting the kids to bed, telling stories and singing their favorite songs but tonight I just went through the motions (Ever done that). I hurriedly read a story to Hannah and turned Jackson's tape on, said my goodnights and I collapsed on the couch. Finally, everyone is settled in for the night. Then I heard footsteps coming down the hall.

"Stop. What do you want?" I asked.

It was my son. "I need some water."

After the water came the need to go to the bathroom, then he needed to tell me something, then Hannah needed some water and she wanted to know if daddy had eaten today. I had just started to sit down again when Jackson called "Mom, I need my tape turned over again." I lost it. "Jackson, go to bed!"

Finally, some peace and quiet, I got settled on the couch once again. Moments later, I felt someone breathing on my face. I didn't even open my eyes. "Go back to bed," I moaned.

Slowly my son turned and walked down the hall a little ways then he turned around and blew me a kiss. "I love you, I just wanted you to know that," he said. Then quietly went into his room and went to bed. That moment froze in my mind and I must have replayed it tens of times. I felt Jesus tell me, "That's how you treat me sometimes. You're to tired to listen to my calling, to tired to spend time with me; but I can renew your strength. You're distracted but I can give you peace. You feel alone but I can fulfill your needs. You feel taken for granted but I love you unconditionally."

Despite my selfish desire to be alone that evening, my son

continued to love me and despite my selfish excuses to spend time with God, he continues to pursue me and love me.

Moment of Encouragement

What a grouch!! I get embarrassed when I read this now. I've grown up a lot since then. However, it's easy to fall back into being self-centered. Kids are very demanding especially at three and five. It's not selfish to want some times to ourselves but we do need to be careful how act before we get it. I have never really given much thought about how I might treat God the same way until that night. What a wake up call. How many times have you felt God calling you to do something or say something to that certain someone and just moaned? We miss lots of blessings with a sour attitude.

Moment with the Father

Heavenly Father, how sorry I am that do not give you the highest priority in my life 100 percent of the time. Help me to learn better ways to structure my day so that I have time with you first and then you can help me organize the other areas of my life that need my time. Also, help me find ways to give myself mini breaks so that I do not feel so burned out. I know with you I can be all that I need to be. Amen.

The Right Road

I am the way, and the truth, and the life; no one comes to the Father but through me. John 14:6

oday my ears were tuned in on your small voices as you talked to each other while we drove around town running errands. "That's a church, Hannah. It's not big like ours but God lives there too," Jackson said.

"Wook, mommy. Dare's daddy's ruck," said Hannah.

"No Hannah, that's just a truck that looks like daddy's," I corrected.

I laugh to myself as the two of you talk. Amazed at the things you see and what you think. I cherish our time we spend traveling around town running errands. I watch other people busy about their day. They're so unaware of the precious conversations I have the privilege of listening to.

"Mom, are we in the right lane?" asked Jackson.

"What do you mean?" I questioned.

"Is this the right road to go get a movie?" he clarified.
"Yes honey," I replied.

Are we going down the right road? What an amazing question. There are several ways I could go to get to our favorite movie rental place. There's a short cut I know to cut through all the traffic lights and stop signs. There's a long way with lots of stops signs and traffic lights and there's another long way with a bit of a scenic view but they all get me to the same place. There are times I wonder, "Jesus am I on the right road of motherhood? There are short cuts to parenting and there are time consuming tasks but not all ways to mothering lead to bringing honor to you. Do my children see you in the way I respond to them? Do they hear your tenderness in my speech? Please let them see the way to you through me."

Moment of Encouragement

The way you mother your child will have an impact on his/her insight to Jesus Christ. All the small, mundane tasks and chores you do each day, caring for your children will impact their lives; so do not grow weary. What you do makes a difference and your children notice what you do but more important than that your Heavenly Father notices.

Moment with the Father

Most gracious Heavenly Father, the task of raising children can be overwhelming and I know each child is a blessing and gift from you. Guide me and give me wisdom as I parent today. Let the things I teach my children bring honor to you and may I prepare my children for the long road ahead. Amen

The Perfect Mother's Day

*Unless the Lord builds the house, they labor
in vain who build it..." Psalm 127:1*

*T*oday I woke early and enjoyed my stroll around the quietness of my household. I secretly entered each of my child's rooms and stared at their faces, watched their breathing and savored the peace of the moment that each one was still, content and quiet. I made me a cup of coffee and glanced out my window to see God greeting me with a warm "Good Morning" by providing a beautiful sunrise. Then I just sat in silence resting in the quietness of my secret place, for I knew all to soon that this same place would suddenly become full of "I needs, I wants, do this, do that" and the demands of the day would begin.

My thoughts were suddenly interrupted by my sixteen month old needing her diaper changed, and then came my husband needing a wrinkle free shirt and a matching sock, my three year old son was thirsty and my coffee was getting cold. I patiently took my daughter and changed her diaper while I directed my husband where he could find a shirt and some socks. I made my way down the hall carrying the baby and directing my son towards the kitchen so I could begin to fix breakfast. I diligently prepared a hot breakfast of eggs, toast, bacon and juice; while my daughter clung to my leg crying and my impatient son asked me "Why you took so long? " (interrupted to mean, "why is it taking you so long to fix me something to eat?). I set the table with one arm, for in the other I now was holding the unhappy baby, and my son had given up on breakfast and was exploring. I knew that would mean a mess to clean up later, after I had made sure everyone was fed. I called that breakfast was ready. Suddenly my husband appeared to announce, "I'm running late honey, I have no time to eat, have a good day, and I love you." I called for my son only to be told, "I not want any eggs". So I fed my daughter and warmed my coffee. My son appears again self-dressed, right down to fixing his bright red hair by using blue, winter fresh toothpaste as hair gel. My daughter had decided to feed her eggs to the cats, but the cats think this is a new toy and begin batting cold eggs around my kitchen floor. My coffee is now cold again. I begin to clear the table of dishes, pick up the uneaten eggs, wipe the toothpaste out of my son's hair, dress my daughter, find a lost matchbox car, and wind a musical toy all before returning to my kitchen where my days chores await. I silently load the dishwasher, wipe the counters, wipe the table and chairs, sweep the floor and read a story, sing a few songs. Then I pass a mirror in the hall and catch a glance of myself; I have not even dressed myself or combed my hair and it's already 10:30am. So I retire to my room close the door and attempt to dress but there before me are two faces staring at me and my son said, "Where are we going?" "No where, mommy's just getting some different clothes on," I reply.

For the remainder of my day I'm followed by two very dependent small people, who watch my every move, hang on my every word. Their world is so small and so innocent. Yet my world seems to overwhelm me and seems so busy. I'm their protector; my eyes and ears filter all things before it reaches their eyes and ears. My job is truly important and a huge responsibility. Most of what I do will go unseen by the world's eyes and the events of my day will likely not make front page news but I wouldn't trade my day for anything. 'Cause everyday I get to make a difference in a small person's life and that's the perfect close to this mother's day.

Moment of Encouragement

It takes great courage to choose to be a stay at home mom. It's not the most popular sought after job in the job market. We do have a real job by choosing to stay home and care for our families. I look at it this way, if I can care for all the tasks that is involved in managing a home and family then my husband is free to be the provider God intended him to be. I love being a stay home mom and I strongly encourage others who do and others who would like to stay home. Mothering lasts a lifetime.

Moment with the Father

Heavenly Father, I'm grateful that I can be a stay home mom and that I can have a lasting influence on my child's life. Thank you that each day I can experience all the wonders of being a mother. Amen.

Happy Birthday, Jackson

*My son give attention to my wisdom, incline your ear to my under-
standing; that you may observe discretion and your lips may
reserve knowledge. Proverbs 5: 1-2*

Jackson Turns One Year Old

*M*y how this year has flew by. I cannot believe you are one
year old today. You're doing so much on your own like
walking, talking, putting puzzles together, making up stories and
songs. You're so smart and it amazes me how quickly you can learn
a new task and how you want to learn everything all at once. You
are always looking for something to do. I love your bright red hair,
your blue eyes and the dimples on your cheeks. I still have a hard
time grasping that you're mine. For so long we wanted a baby and I
was beginning to think it wasn't meant to be and then God so
graciously blessed us with you. You were due to be born on
Christmas day but decided to come one day late. So planning future

birthday parties is going to be quite unique. It's been quite a year to remember. You haven't been the easiest baby but I'm learning you're just very frustrated because you want to do many things that developmentally your body is not ready for. Your mind is a bit ahead of the rest of you. You cry a lot and get very angry when you don't get your way but I'm also very stubborn and there have been days you and I battled it out. But all in all, I love you and I'm so glad to have you in our family.

Jackson Turns Two Years Old

You're two today and everyone knows it. You're very active and independent and do not want anyone to help you with anything. You're favorite phrase is "I do it all myself". You sang Happy Birthday to Jesus yesterday and I just cried. No one told you to you just came up with the idea own your own. You enjoy playing with little matchbox cars that you call "cool cars" and you have a special box you keep them in. If one goes missing you know, I don't know how but you do. You enjoy playing a game you made up called "push down" with daddy. It's a game that you will only play with him if I try to play it you quickly tell me "you not play it like daddy, you can't play". I get the privilege to sing to you at night though.

Jackson Turns Three Years Old

Well, you're a big brother this year. We welcomed Hannah Elizabeth into our family. You have been so patient with her and I love to watch you go secretly into her room and place one of your valued "cool cars" into her crib. It's very obvious that you care for her. You've changed so much in a year and your knowledge about your surroundings and world has just vastly increased. You ask such detailed questions about Jesus and you're so aware of his presence in our lives it amazes me. You have such a tender heart and yet you're so set in your ways. I just know you're going to a leader of some kind when you grow up. You have all the characteristics. You keep me busy answering lots and lots of questions. Some I have to think about before I answer you and you get very impatient with me. You're very special and I love the young man you're becoming.

I desire for you to know that you're loved every day and I'm here to help you in any way I can throughout your life. I want you to feel secure enough with our relationship that you trust me enough to share with me anything good and bad and as problems arise (which I'm sure they will) we can work together to find a solution. I desire for you to understand that Jesus is always by your side even when I can't be and in time of need all you need to do in trust in him and call on his name and I promise you he'll show up. I hope that you will be able to see the work of Jesus in my life as you continue to grow so that you will see a visual example of God's sovereignty. I love you, Jackson. Love, Mama

This is my prayer to you: *I do not cease giving thanks for you, while making mention of you in my prayers that the God of our Lord Jesus Christ, the Father of glory, may give to you a spirit of wisdom and of revelation in the knowledge of Him. I pray that the eyes of your heart may be enlightened, so that you will know what is the hope of His calling, what are the riches of the glory of His inheritance in the saints, and what is the surpassing greatness of His power toward us who believe. Amen.*

Moment of Encouragement

Birthdays are great and I love to celebrate in a big way. I decided to start writing birthday letters to Jackson so that he would have a record of all the things happening in his life each year. It's a great time to look back and see how he's grown but more than that it's a time I look back on myself and see how I've to grown. Our children are not the only ones celebrating milestones in their lives, we as mothers are too. Each passing year we learn more effective ways to draw ourselves closer to our children and in turn God shows us ways to draw ourselves closer to him.

Moment with the Father

Heavenly Father, I thank you for Jackson. I'm so proud to be his mama. He's the most beautiful baby I ever saw and I just love his red hair. That was a special touch from you, only you can design that color of red. Jackson has so many wonderful qualities and his personality is truly one of a kind. I know you have awesome plans for him. I pray you will bless him and place your crown of favor upon his head. I pray you will guide me as his mother to teach and train him in your ways and that he will live a purpose that brings honor and glory to you. Amen

It's Me, Again

Be sober in all things, endure hardship, do the work of an evangelist, fulfill your ministry. II Timothy 4:5

*L*ord, it's me again. This must be the eighth time this morning. Lord, I just needed to make sure you're still here and that the terrible two's and the make believe batman saving the world didn't run you off. I know it's noisy these days in our home but bear with me. Lord, my "to do list" is unending, everything I have listed needs to be done first and nothing has gotten done; it's already 10:30am and lunch is drawing near. I'm usually more organized than this but today I seem to be having trouble getting things prioritized. Lord, how did Mary do it? Was she the perfect mother, never fretting, always available, never tiring and always patient? If I just knew all that I'm doing is making a difference. My little ones just don't seem to care that there is four loads of dirty clothes waiting to be washed, the frig needs cleaning, the toilets need a good scrubbing, the glass doors need wiping (lots of sticky fingers), bills need paying. Oh, I laugh when I think about how I thought I would be bored and have too much time on my hands when I decided to stay home. Most days there are just not enough hours in the day to do all that is required of me. I don't really get a break or a day off and I can forget any kind of sick days. Lord, bless all stay home moms today. Touch all of us and give us endless strength and boundless patience to face our battles.

This is what God showed me:

With each spill I clean, I thank God for overlooking each childish mistake I make

With each dirty face I wipe clean, I thank God for wiping my sins away and for remembering them never again.

With each lost shoe I find, I thank God he cares about me enough to never leave nor forsake me.

With each child I console, I thank God that I can go to him anytime, anywhere and as many times as I need

With each "I can do it, myself" even when I can see my help is needed, I thank God he never gives up on me and accepts me no matter what

With each day that passes and I don't see the difference I'm making, I thank God that he can and because His grace is sufficient I can look forward to another day of becoming the mother God wants my children to have.

Moment of Encouragement

Wow! I still get goose bumps when I read that. God revealed so plainly the little things I do for my children are the same daily little things, tiring things, mundane things he does for me. God never tires of hearing from you, go to him today. Tell him about your day; he cares for you.

Moment with the Father

Heavenly Father, I'm in awe of your love for me. I cannot begin to understand how you never rest, never get weary, never get impatient. Thank you for making a way for me to come to you and cast my cares at your feet. Amen.

My Mission Field

*T*onight was my last night teaching mission friends at our church. I'll miss teaching and singing to those four year olds. I taught for three years and although the need is still there for more teachers in our church, I felt a deeper calling. I feel there are so many mothers that serve in their churches, charity organizations, sporting events, school events and clubs that we miss out on the most important area to serve – our family. I've often thought that by being a stay home mom my witnessing and serving God would not exist until my children were older but God has shown me that the greatest mission field is telling my children about him, setting a godly example for their eyes to see, caring for their montone needs with gladness, being merciful with their childish mistakes. A mother's mission field is not miles away or poverty stricken and it may seem like such a simple small world to minister to but the need is so very great and so very important to our God. Let's don't miss out on the greatest mission adventure ever by neglecting to notice the difference we make in serving our children. It's the world's largest mission field – Motherhood.

Moment of Encouragement

I'm going to step onto my soapbox for a moment so bear with me. I've seen too many women take on tasks like MOPS, Mission Friends, children's choir, adult choir, organizing home school events, coaching, mentoring, and the list could go on and on. It's great for a while and then the responsibility of it all takes its toll and you begin to feel overwhelmed. All these tasks are great, don't get me wrong, I've served in many of these functions and likely will again. It's just that, I don't want women to miss the one true place to serve that will make a lasting impact - which is their family. There are times we need to serve and then there are times we need to make the call and set the boundaries.

Moment with the Father

Dear Heavenly Father, at times I feel the duties I perform as a mother are not counting for much. Please help me see the differences I make in my little ones lives. Give me courage and strength as I face my many responsibilities each day. Guide me in finding teachable moments to tell my children about you. Help me to discern when to say yes and when to say no to other areas of service. Amen

I Don't Want to be a Mommy Today!

Whoever receives one child like this in my name receives me...
Mark 9:37

I was awaken by tiny eyes staring and a whispering voice saying "Mommy, mommy open your eyes. Get me some chocolate milk." Then a bang that would give new meaning to the "Big Bang" theory truly got my attention and so I got out of my warm, cozy bed and headed down the hall. Tiny feet behind me and a panic four year old running towards me making his confession " I didn't do it! I-I-I was jjjjust trying....". "Mommy, chocolate milk!" claims my two-year-old daughter once again. I make it to the kitchen and gaze around, unwashed dishes lay in the sink, pieces of unwanted paper wait to be thrown away, a whole gallon milk has been left sitting on the counter (likely all night), the cat is eating my favorite plant, there's no coffee to be found and suddenly I hear the sound of water rushing. "Mommy, get me my chocolate milk!" screams my impatient daughter. "I wet my bed mama, I'm sorry but I put my sheets in the washer for you," boasts my son. "And I used the good smelling dish soap." Did he say DISH soap?!

Oh, Lord, I don't want to be a mommy today. Can I call in today pleeeassse and use a sick day. I know if I hurry, I can still make it back to my bed and it'll still be warm. I'll give up my hot cup of coffee. Just call in a replacement for me today and I'm sure I'll be better able to cope tomorrow. Thanks a lot Lord and by the way tell my replacement I said, "GOOD LUCK!"

Moment of Encouragement

I cannot begin to count how many days I had begin like this one. Although funny now, it wasn't at the time. Maybe you find you're having one of those days today. It's not always fun, rewarding, and glamorous being a mom but you are. You are a GREAT mother!!!

Moment with the Father

Heavenly Father, there are times when each day seems to be a replay of this kind of day. I don't want to be a mommy always. I'd like to sleep late sometimes or just go have a day of fun. I know you are aware of my needs and wants and so I turn them over to you right now and I ask you to give me the desire to be a mommy today. Amen.

Privileges

*How blessed are those who observe His testimonies who seek Him
with all their heart. Psalm 119:1-2*

I've been thinking a lot today about being a mother and just
what all that involves. I know I take care of the kids and keep
the house clean but I do a whole lot more than just those two things.
It's a courageous choice but I like to think of it as a privilege. I've
thought about what are some of the daily things that seem to
become a bothersome kind of chore and things that make a change
in the life God blessed me with. So here's my list:

To be awaken at 2:08am for feeding time and to hear the peaceful
sounds of the world at rest.
To be awaken again at 5:17am for feeding time and to see God
wake up the world.
To be greeted with smiles and drool
To be called ma-ma for the first time and to then hear that word

develop into different pitches

To fix a meal that only gets two bites eaten

To fill sippy cups at least ten times before lunch

To clean five spills one of which happens just before you're ready to walk out the door

To be the first and last image your child sees

To go all day without changing from your pjs into regular clothes simply because you didn't have time

To forget to comb your hair

To fall so deep in love with a small demanding, sometimes cranky, bald "prince charming"

To look forward to spending another day with that same person

To be the first play mate

To help button a shirt

To brush a little girl's long curly hair

To help tie a shoe nine times within two hours

To build a tent out of blankets and sheets inside and tell stories

To scratch a back a bed time

To sing a favorite song

To have a shadow without the sun making it

To feel the heartbreaks

To have someone to dream for

To be the first to show the love of family

To be the first example of Jesus small eyes see

To watch that person learn more about Jesus and then lead him/she to a personal relationship with the Heavenly Father

To enable someone to become independent and walk in the ways of Jesus

To make a lasting influence

To experience the deepest kind of love there is

These are the privileges of motherhood. Our job is challenging and tiring but with much that is given much is required.

Moment of Encouragement

Sure there are times that reading one more story becomes just a chore but a look of appreciation from that face you've fallen in love with can change that chore until a long awaited privilege. Our children are a blessing from God and the bothersome things they request from us are really hidden privileges that we seem to not notice. Don't think you are not making a difference in your child's life because you are; you're just not seeing it all. Take notice today.

Moment with the Father

Heavenly Father, I'm so glad that you helped me take notice of these things that I do and they really are privileges that most people do not get a chance to experience. Help me not to overlook the small blessings you put in my path each day. I want so badly to remember each moment of being a mother. Amen.

The Power of Love and Mercy

In my distress I called upon the Lord,
and cried to my God for help; He heard my
voice out of His temple, and my
cry for help before Him came into His ears. Psalm 18:6

I was awaken by the sound of whining and grunting, no words, only whining and grunting. When asked what was wrong, I only got more but louder whining and grunting. Still lying in bed I could feel my insides begin to churn, I knew I had a mountain to climb today bigger than Mount Everest. My four-year-old son was telling me he did not want to go to school, the same school that yesterday he didn't want to leave. I hugged, talked to, encouraged, and prayed with this child but now the whining had turned to crying and soon I knew screaming would meet me at the first summit.

Breakfast anyone? The bowl of Fruit Loops I had fixed my son was untouched. My son was on the kitchen floor crying. My 2-year-old daughter was happily eating her cereal while the cats played chase around my son. "God, give me strength, help me to know what to do," I prayed. The climb to the next summit was beginning. I was fighting my son to get his clothes on which can give new meaning to a "cage wrestling match". "More loop, loops" cried my daughter from the kitchen. Oh, I nearly forgot that I had another child. I return to the kitchen and dish out more cereal. "Tank you" and a smile was her reply. "Thank you God, for this piece of comfort," I prayed. Back in my son's room, I continue to fight with him to get him dressed. I had made it the second summit; the child's clothes were now officially on. Now, to get everyone safely in the van. Oh, what fun this is going to be. "God, please help me do this. Help Jackson feel my love and help him cooperate with me," I prayed. I got Hannah buckled in her car seat and headed back in the house to find Jackson. I knew he would be hiding. I chased him through the house and finally grabbed him. Kicking, screaming and hitting I carried him to the van. Boy, this is not fun, I thought as we made our way towards the van. I hope the neighbors are gone. Finally I got everyone in the van. Here we go to school. "God, it's me again. How much more screaming does he have in him? Oh, please hear my cries for your help. My heart is breaking. Give Jackson strength today." Lots and lots of screaming and crying were endured all the way to school. We make it to the school. "Thank you God, for helping me tolerate his screams."

Now, to get him into the school and to his classroom. I open the van's door. Oh, great (although I wanted to say something else), he has taken his shoes off!! Now the climb to the third summit is about to begin and oh the joys that await me. I sit on the doorframe of the van, my son lying back in my arms, my legs are wrapped around one foot while the other foot is kicking me in the face. I get one shoe on and tied when the other shoe is kicked off again and thrown into the parking lot. About that time a parent leaving, backs up and runs over my son's shoe! "Dear God, I sure could use some help here. Where are you? Have you ran away? I know I want to, please do not leave me here alone to handle this," I prayed.

I watched as parents and kids happily walked into school and here I sat with my son's body in positions that didn't seem possible while he kicked and screamed. I finally got his shoes on then I took him in my arms, "I love you, I love you, I love you Jackson," I say as I fight with every ounce of strength in my body to not cry. "Wing, wing ma-ma. I go wing," states Hannah. She's been watching the children on the playground playing all this time. I gather her in one arm and Jackson in the other, and off we go. Once inside the school I put Jackson down, POOF! off he runs. (The child's persistent). Someone catches him. Parents and children are everywhere. All eyes and ears are on me, people are whispering and my heart feels like it's going to burst from the embarrassment and hurt. I want to take my child and run – run as far away as I can from this place and never return. I'm frozen. What do I do now? What do I say? A teacher takes my son and looks at me, "He'll be fine," she states. "No. No. Mommy!" is what I hear as I exit the building. Tears begin to fall as I make it to the van. I had climbed Mount Everest, the top of the world, and here I sit alone, embarrassed and hurting. I cried. "Lord, I don't know what to do, I don't know what to say or pray about in this situation. My son is hurting and so am I. This tough love thing stinks!! I'm tired of all the whining, crying and screaming. I'm tired of all the cruel looks from people. They don't have a clue what it's like to have such a strong willed child nor do they know how hard I'm trying to do what is right. I've been patient, I've waited and I've tolerated but now I'm tired- very tired. I'm so confused and hurt and I need you to fix me. Hide me Lord and give me rest. So, I sat there and wept. I wept for all the mothers that are trying to do right by their children but don't see any progress yet. I wept for all mothers who feel alone and afraid. I wept for mothers who have strong willed children, like myself, that face challenges like this one every day. It was quite on the drive back home as I thought about what had happen. It was only 8:30am and I had already climbed a mountain.

Moment of Encouragement

I struggled with sharing this story in this book but I felt it was important to those mothers of high spirited, strong willed children to show what your day can be like. I know I'm not the only mother out there that's got a story like this one. I know some of you may be thinking "thank you, God" for not giving me a child like that while others of you are thinking "thank you, God that I'm not the only one who struggles with a strong willed child". Yes, strong willed children are born that way; they are not raised that way. Trust me I have tried many times to change my son's strong willed ways but you can not change a trait that was given by our God Almighty. These are the people that invent things, run huge companies, get things done and they're few and far between. They are highly intelligent humans that think totally outside the box. So therefore, you have to parent outside the box. Be patient with these kids and keep their mothers' in your prayers.

Moment with the Father

Heavenly Father, thank you for the kind of child I have. Thank you that you are so creative in your design of each personality. Although, some people are harder to understand and get along with than others; these are the very things that can give spice to our dull lives. Thank you for going with me as I learn better ways to parent this child you richly blessed me with. Amen.

The Rest of the Story

For My thoughts are not your thoughts,
neither are your ways
My ways, declares the Lord,...
Isaiah 55:8

*N*ow for the rest of the story; I hope you don't think that was all there was to that horrible morning. (Note to readers: first read The Power of Love and Mercy). It's now the afternoon and time for me to pick up my son. It seems like years since this morning but it's only been 6 hours. His teacher called me to let me know he did calm down. I wonder what kind of day he had. I think I've asked all the questions, mothers must ask themselves when they have preschoolers: Am I doing the right thing? Is it really necessary that he have time away from me?

God, is it possible that you can make an exception to the rule of this part of growing up and let us just skip over this part? (Only in my dreams) I made it to the parking lot of the school and as I sat there I thought about all that had transpired today. I had learned a valuable lesson about love - not just any love - but the unconditional, sacred love of a mother for her child. Jackson, how I wish you could feel the love that overflows from my heart. There's nothing that you could do to quench it and despite the morning we shared my love for you has only grown. God chose me of all the women in the world, he chose me, to be your mommy. I consider it an honor to be the one a God chose to raise you. Today has been a day that there was only one set of footprints in the sand. God carried me today.

The school bell ringing interrupts my thoughts; I watch with anticipation – there he is. We slowly walk towards one another and then I begin to walk faster and he picks up speed too. I gather him in my arms and whisper "I sure did miss you today, I love you so." We both start to laugh and as we walk back to the van he squeezes my hand and says, "I like it best when I'm home with you, mommy." I hold him close and whisper, "I know, so do I."

Moment of Encouragement

There are times in mothering that it's encouraging to know that God's ways are not our ways. God has a much better outlook on things than we do and his plans for our lives are much better than we could ever imagine. I find that encouraging especially with my children because he knows the plans he has for them and if I trust in him he can direct my ways to be in step with his ways.

Moment with the Father

Heavenly Father, I'm so grateful to you for the plans you have for me as a mother and a wife. If my desires are not in tune with your ways I pray you will change me. I so much want what is best for my children and I know you have great plans for them. Help guide me as I mother so that I can raise these children to bring honor to you. Amen.

To be Me Again

To You, O Lord, I call; My rock, do not be deaf to me, For if you are silent to me, I will become like those who go down to the pit. Hear the voice of my supplications when I cry to You for help.
Psalm 28:1-2

*G*od, you're silent today and I don't understand why. I don't feel your presence in this place as I stand here with another day to:

Wash clothes, sweep a floor, wipe a face, change a child's wet clothes (trying to potty train child #2), make a peanut butter and jelly sandwich, tie a shoe, find a lost doll, rewind a movie, feed the cats, pay the electric bill, take out the garbage, wipe sticky hands, play a game, fill a sippy cup with juice, tie a shoe (again), wash dishes, make three beds, find a lost sock, read a story, answer questions and more questions, change a child's wet clothes (again), fix 3 lunches, wash dishes (again), find a misplaced super hero, stop a fight among brother and sister....

Oh, my Lord, is there something more, something I'm missing out on outside these walls? I wonder. Today my world seems so small, so boring, so confining, and so NOT what I wanted. God I long for your touch today. These walls are closing in and the monotony of it all is more than I can take. Everyone is so needy and demanding. I want to close my eyes and just disappear for a while. I'd like to wash my hair without stopping twice to stop a fight and get soap in my eyes while I'm doing it; I'd like to eat a meal without sharing any portions from my plate or saying "stop that, say please, don't spit at the table, use your napkin not your sleeve"; I'd like to drink a cup of coffee while it's hot; I'd like to sit quietly for 15 minutes without having to get up and do absolutely nothing; I'd like to smell pretty without the linger of the smell of baby wipes or diaper rash oinment; I'd like to get dressed without any interruptions or "little spies"; I'd like to feel appreciated and respected ; I'd like to feel like more than just a mother. I'd like to feel like me again.

Moment of Encouragement

Do you sometimes get lost in being a mother and doing all the things mothers do that you forget the real person you are. I've always had the dream of writing and getting a book published. I've always thought after reading other authors books "I can write that good, why can't I get my work published?" Then somewhere the dream gets misplaced and soon another dream gets misplaced and then a certain hobby gets put on hold and before long you're not sure what your purpose is. God has a purpose for each one us and trust me he knows each one of your dreams, desires and hobbies. He can help you find them and begin anew. It's not selfish to want to do a thing that you enjoy that's what makes us who we are and God wants you to enjoy life to the fullest. I encourage you to pick something that you really want to do and make a plan to carry it out. It can be as simple as taking a hot bath without interruptions or as glamorous as getting a massage. Just do it.

<u>Moment with the Father</u>

Heavenly Father, being woman is very difficult at times. We are emotional creatures that demand a lot of love and understanding often times when we do not deserve it. In providing care to our family it is easy to lose sight of who we are and our likes and dislikes. Thank you that you are always intimately acquainted with our thoughts and desires and with your help we can see our wildest dreams come true. Amen.

Christmas Presents

For I know the plans I have for you, declares the Lord, plans for welfare and not for calamity to give you a future and a hope.
Jeremiah 29:11

*J*oy overflows my soul as I see the excitement on your faces this Christmas season. As I place presents wrapped neatly under the tree you run relaying the event that another gift has been wrapped and placed under the tree.

"Look, what's in this one mommy?" Your eyes wide with excitement hoping I will reveal the secret.

"Oh, I wonder," pretending not to know.

Carefully you pick it up give a little shake. "Can we open it now?" you plead with me.

"You have to wait until Christmas," I reply knowing the next question before you ask.

"How many more days is that?" you say.

"Seventeen," I reply.

"That's forty five, six billion and two days. That will take to long," you huff.

"No, seventeen days is not that long. It will be here sooner than you think," I try to explain, but you're now pleading and whining to open just one present and sharing with me your opinions of how unfair it is that I know what's in the present.

"If I tell you, it'll spoil the surprise," I say as I try to reason with a three year old.

"No it won't! I'm going to open it when you're not looking," you protest.

I walk away knowing this not a battle I want to fight right now. You stay at the Christmas tree looking at the gifts and huffing.

As I finish wrapping presents, I realize how my life is a lot like these gifts. God has each day of my life wrapped up and placed in a certain place to be unwrapped at the right time. He knows what's in each package and knows what my reaction will be. But how many times do I go before him, much like my son coming to me, pleading, begging and questioning. Children have a hard time understanding the concept of time and what only is a little while seems like an eternity to them. Yet, I have the same problem understanding God's timetable. How often does God try to reassure us by saying I know you're anxious but I know what you need and I know the perfect time, be patient and wait on me?

<u>Moment of Encouragement</u>

It's so hard for me to keep surprises but yet I love being surprised. I can keep a secret most of the time but it is a real struggle. God has so many surprises wrapped up for you and me and yet he has no trouble keeping them a secret. His vision is so much greater than ours. So the next time you find yourself impatient with an unanswered request, remember God has it covered and Christmas day may not be as long as you think.

Moment with the Father

Heavenly Father, thank you for your vision and the plans you have ordained for me. I get impatient when things don't happen when and how I want them to. It's hard for me to always see things like you want me to but I do desire to. Amen.

Happy Birthday, Hannah

If you seek her as silver and search for her as for hidden treasures;
then you will discern the fear of the lord and discover the knowl-
edge of God. Proverbs 2: 4-5

Hannah turns one year old

*T*oday is your birthday and it's hard for me to believe that you're one. I cannot begin to tell you how much you've changed my life. God has blessed me with a precious little girl with curly hair and bright blue eyes. I love your smile, the way you want only me some days, the way you chatter away whether someone is listening or not, and the way you love your daddy. You brighten my day and I'm so glad that God blessed our family with you. I enjoy the time you and I spend at bedtime rocking and I wish I could bottle the smell of you. Your daddy thinks that I spend way to long holding you after you've fallen to sleep but I know you're my last baby and I won't get the chance to do all these things again. So, for now I'm like a giant sponge soaking up each moment. I'll admit I've spoiled you to a point but I love you so and my heart feels that it will burst at times.

You're trying really hard to walk but prefer to crawl instead. You enjoy listening to music and try to dance. You love to dress up in anything you can get your hands on. You love to run through the house naked (what baby doesn't). You love playing with Jackson.

Hannah turns two years old

You're two today and my how you've changed. You're suddenly so independent and think you can do everything without any help from me. Oh where did my baby go? "No! and I do it!" are you're favorite phrases. You love chocolate milk, cheese eggs, peanut butter and jelly, pickles with ketchup, and you have discovered what happy meals are. You have developed a wonderful friendship with a child that I keep during the day named Hannah also. Most days the two of you are inseparable. You've become your T-Da's (grandfather) shadow and trust me he loves it. You enjoy helping me bake cakes, singing, reading stories, playing games, and playing with dolls. You also love to climb onto the dishwasher door as I'm putting the dishes away and each time the frig is opened you love to sit on the ledge inside.

Hannah turns three years old

Well, look who turns three today. We celebrated with a princess party and lots of family and friends enjoyed the castle cake and making their own crowns. You looked like a little princess. You're getting so big and you're personality is in full bloom. You speak your mind and are very persistent. You and Jackson have had some interesting debates some of which I don't think are over. You love to play dress up and have your picture taken. You like to have time to yourself and find some strange places to hide and play. But I can relate better to that than daddy and so I don't mind having to search for you. I've found you under your bed, in the closet, behind chairs and under tables. I guess our biggest struggle we have at this time is pottying. You really have no desire to have dry clothes and it makes me crazy. I do a lot of washing. You like to invent your own little world and get lost in it. I look at as being very creative. It's just a special characteristic that God gave you. You're becoming aware of who Jesus is and that he cares for you. I love the questions you ask and the way you get words confused. You're so innocent. And I love you more each day.

I desire for you to know and feel my love each day. I want to be a parent to you first and a friend to you second. The whole point of being a mother is to train you in what's right and to teach you to walk in God's ways. I desire to build a relationship with you where you will not fear coming to me about anything. I want you to know that Jesus is our one and only provider and without him we are nothing. He can get you through anything. I love you, Hannah. Love, Mama

This is my prayer to you: *I do not cease giving thanks for you, while making mention of you in my prayers that the God of our Lord Jesus Christ, the Father of glory, may give to you a spirit of wisdom and of revelation in the knowledge of Him. I pray that the eyes of your heart may be enlightened, so that you will know what is the hope of His calling, what are the riches of the glory of His inheritance in the saints, and what is the surpassing greatness of His power toward us who believe. Amen.*

Moment of Encouragement

I try very hard to write a letter to each of my children on their birthday and try to include things like: their interests, accomplishments, friendships, funny things they say, special stories that happened, struggles that we had and overcome, my desires and a brief summary of that year. It's a great way to keep track of the many changes that occur over time and hopefully one day they will enjoy reading them. I encourage you to give it a try.

Moment with the Father

Heavenly Father, thank you for Hannah. She's such a blessing and I'm so honored you chose her to be a part of our family. You've given her so many talents and a great imagination there's no telling how she will use it. Your gift of life still amazes me. I pray she will grow to develop a personal relationship with you and that she will look to you for final guidance and direction in her life. I know you have awesome plans for her and I pray you will help me as I teach and train her to bring honor and glory to you in all that she accomplishes. Amen.

Jury Duty

All the ways of a man are clean in his own sight, but the Lord weighs the motives. Commit your works to the Lord and your plans will be established. Proverbs 16:2-3

For the first time ever I was called to my citizen duty – jury duty. It was more cumbersome for our family than for others because I am the sole caregiver for our children. My husband made arrangements to take off from his job to take my place and care for the kids while I attended jury selection. He was praying I didn't get picked and I was unsure what I wanted. Part of me wanted to get picked so I could have a break from the daily chores of home and part of me just wanted to stay home. I went over our basic schedule for a normal day with my husband and made sure he understood how things were to be handled in my absence. The day came for me to go. Wow, what a strange feeling this is, getting up, getting dressed up and only having to take care of myself. I'm feeling a bit lost. I gather my belongings and head out the door. Then I see two pair of eyes; two pair of hands and two faces smooched to the glass door. I bow kisses and wave good-bye. Whew! I made it. Free. Free at last. As I drive to the courthouse my mind is filled with many thoughts: "Oh, I'm so glad I don't have to deal with this traffic every day; how I hate panty hose and dress shoes. The scene of my two children's faces pressed against the glass fills my head and suddenly I realize the most important duty is waiting for me at home.

Moment of Encouragement

I didn't get picked for jury duty and after it was all over; I was really glad. I got the best welcome home cheer when I returned. Sometimes it's a good thing when we have other duties to attend to other than our mothering. It can be a time to reflect on the many blessings you have at your disposal each day but sometimes forget. Such as, staying in your pjs all day because you don't want to get dressed or running bare-footed in the yard.

Moment with the Father

Heavenly Father, help me not to forget the blessings I have at home. It's so easy to forget and lots of times I do. I'm grateful that you have provided a way for me to take care of my family full time. Amen.

The Rocking Chair

Sing for joy in the Lord, O you righteous ones;
Praise is becoming to the upright. Sing to Him a new song;
play skillfully with a shout of joy. Psalm 33:1 & 3

*E*veryone is sleeping and here I am before you, my Lord, hiding my face at your feet. How great and awesome are you, O God. I praise you. How blessed I am. Our Jackson starts school tomorrow he's ready, but I'm not (is any mother ready for her child to start school?). My heart aches as he makes yet another step away from my care. Yes, Lord, I know he does not belong to me; he's just on loan from you.

He approached me so sweetly tonight and asked, "Mama would you rock me?" "Sure," I replied.

Lord, this is the same child that could not be comforted in any way imaginable as a baby. Above all other things he hated to be rocked. Time has yet to help me forget those days. Now here he is six years old and curled up in my lap. We rocked, talked and he stroked my face. "I love you, Mama. Can you sing to me?" he said. "Any special requests?" I asked. "Amazing Grace," he smiled. I sang and he closed his eyes and relaxed. I continued to rock him long after he fell asleep, wanting to remember this moment forever.

I can not count how many times I had sung Amazing Grace to him as a baby, hoping to calm him if only for a few seconds of quiet. Maybe now that I look back I sang more to myself than to him so as to comfort my own soul. Nevertheless, the song somehow left an impression on his heart. Oh, my Lord, how unworthy I am to receive such an honor as this tonight. Only you, my Lord, know what it means to me for Jackson to make such a simple request. I've waited six years to have this privilege; the privilege to rock my baby. And you, O God, have seen to it. Thank you, for Jackson; he's such a joy to my life. I'm so honored you chose me to be his mommy. How wonderful are your thoughts of me that you would entrust such a child as this into my care. I cannot express to you my gratitude for a richer gift. My heart breaks that my mothering to him is changing and the little boy I once knew will be no more. My strongest desire is for him to be a light for you. Thanks again for my time in the rocking chair.

Moment of Encouragement

It's hard to see our kids venture out of our nests for the first time. You have an odd feeling of bitter sweetness about your day. (I think I just made up a word but I like it. All you grammar people out there over look it.) Anyway, this was a tough time for me. I knew I was going to have a tough time with Jackson and although I had considered home schooling I just did not feel God calling me to do that at this time. I felt Jackson needed the structure and socializing that a school setting can give. I applaud all those of you who do home school. I have many friends who do and they often have encouraged me to as well and have been available to answer questions I had. After lots of praying we decided it was best to enroll him in school and so the day came and I wept. He's done great and has even skipped a grade. But the lesson I learned in all this was that because I was faithful during the hard times when Jackson did not want to comforted God chose to bless me with a far richer blessing than I could have ever imagined. If you're struggling with a certain issue with your child today, do not give up. Your blessing might be just another day away and believe me it's well worth the wait.

Moment with the Father

Heavenly Father, I thank you for the different seasons of our lives and how we grow through each one. I'm so grateful that I was able to be at home with Jackson for the past six years and to see him venture off to school. I'm in awe that you would bless me so after all this time with such a special moment as tonight. It offers great encouragement to me as I struggle in other areas of my life. Amen.

Marks of Mothering

Our people must also learn to engage in good deeds to meet pressing needs, so that they will not be unfruitful. Titus 3:14

*L*ord, you're eyes did not miss the events of my day nor did you leave my side and for that I praise your name. I rest in the fact you saw and felt my pain and you caught the pieces of my heart as it was breaking. I'm confident that the staring and whispering I endured today will one day bring glory to your name for you alone are worthy. I could not mother this child you so richly blessed me with if you were not at my beckon call. He's only a little boy but oh how he tests every part of my being! He spit on me, told me I was mean, he pulled my hair and growled at me today Lord!! I felt his hatred but Lord he must go to school and he must learn to be submissive to others in authority. This to shall pass, all in your time for your word said there is a time for every thing and to every thing there is a purpose. It is so hard for me to endure day after day. As I look back over the past few years I've seen myself grow as a mother and today for the first time I was able to look at today's events as marks of my mothering. I've had the stretch marks to prove my body-endured child bearing. I've had the dark circles and bags under my eyes as marks of sleepless nights staying up with a sick child. I've had a tear stained face as marks of frustration, weariness and unfailing love for my child. I've had to say no to my selfish desires and put my dreams on hold and think of my child's needs above my own. And today, I was spit on, called names and stared at for trying to teach my child in your ways, oh Lord. I'm sure there will be more marks of mothering to come but you will go before me and behind me and I shall not fail. I'm greatly comforted when I think of you and the marks you endured, the stares, spiting and name calling you endured for me on Calvary so that I could be forgiven, redeemed and become a mighty child of God. And I find peace and strength in your promise of returning again as I stand before you and you look at my marks of mothering I hope you can pleased enough to say, "Well done my faithful servant."

Moment of Encouragement

I endured a lot of stares and whispers when Jackson was younger simply because he had his own way he wanted to do things despite my guidance. It's called being very strong willed. But, I've learned over the years of parenting Jackson that God is molding me to be a better mother and to encourage other mothers who are just getting started in mothering a strong willed child. God does not allow us to go through tough times in our parenting without having a better outcome. I cannot promise you, you will always understand or see the result of your struggles but just know that God has an awesome plan and you were a major part of it.

Moment with the Father

Gracious Heavenly Father, I'm so overwhelmed of how you suffered for me. The struggles I go through can never compare to what you endured. I do get discouraged at times during my days of mothering because everyone gets demanding and everyone's needs seem to come before my own (how selfish of me). I ask you to take care of my needs today. I commit all my struggles over to you and I ask you to fill my cup. Thank you for making me a mother and thank you for being with me each step of the way. I am comforted knowing that you go before me and behind me and you work all things for the good. Amen.

The Love of Mama

We have not ceased to pray for you and to ask that you may be filled with the knowledge of His will in all spiritual wisdom and understanding, so that you will walk in a manner worthy of the Lord, to please Him in all respects, bearing fruit in every good work and increasing in the knowledge of God. Colossians 1:9-10

I'm missing my mama today. Yes, at the age of 30 something I still long for my mama's touch. There's a special bond that I believe God gives between a mother and a child and no matter what the span of years, the bond remains complete. My mama and I have a very close relationship and I cherish it more and more. There are things that only mama can understand and there are things that only mama can make right again. Mama can just call my name and my heart is calmed. I didn't always agree with my mama especially during the teenage years, frankly I saw her as the enemy but what teenager doesn't. But, now I realize she was called to be my mother first and then my friend and that is a very hard job. We all want our children to like and love us but when we deny them something they desire, suddenly there seems to be a break in the relationship. I look back at times that I was ungrateful and so unworthy of my mother's love but you know she never wavered. She just kept on loving me and leading me along. Her strength came from the same source that I now draw my strength from – Jesus Christ. She sacrificed her desires and dreams to help me accomplish mine. She spent hours in prayer, some times in the middle of the night, praying just for me. Even today as I write this, I know she has already prayed for me. I desire for my children to feel the depth of my love just as I have had the honor to feel the depth of my mother's love. I am what I am today because of your love and devotion. I love you, Mama. All the miles in the world are not to far for the love of mama to reach her child.

Closing Prayer

Finally, brethren, farewell, Mend your ways, heed my appeal, agree with one another, live in peace, and the God of love and peace will be with you. 2 Corinthians 13:11

*W*hat a journey this has been. I once only dreamed of a book to call my own and now here it is. I'm so humbled by the honor to have the talent to put my stories into words for others to read. This book would have never came to be without my deliver, my strong tower, my Savior Jesus Christ. I have enjoyed every step taken to make this happen in hopes to encourage my fellow readers. And so as I close this chapter in my life I offer this prayer to you and your family.

Heavenly Father, how great you are and what an awesome example you set before us as mothers on how we should love and care for our families. Thank you for the perfect instruction manual – your holy word. Thank you for each mother that has this book in her possession and I ask you to bless her, strengthen her and lift her up, hold her steadfast and do not allow her feet to stumble. Whisper your words of hope in her heart, sing to her a new song of grace, and direct her steps each day as she cares for the family you ordained for her. Enable her for the tasks you have for her. Allow her to celebrate in your vastness of wisdom and grace. Thank you for making her a mother. I ask that you allow her to see and reflect on all the moments she will experience as a mommy. In Jesus' Precious and Holy name, Amen.

I would love to hear from you and you can reach me at: Charlotte@RaisedatHome.com
Be blessed.

Printed in the United States
18176LVS00002B/271-462